God's Poetic Path

Our Journey Home
to His Embrace

Dain Scherber, L.C.

Dedicated to the Love of my life: the Lord, who has filled me with the joy of his love and received so little in return from this son of his. Thank you, Jesus.

And to my Mother, the Blessed Virgin Mary, who has never failed to protect and care for me under her mantle.

A special thanks to my parents, my siblings, and my brothers and sisters in the Regnum Christi Movement, who have accompanied and supported me my whole journey.

CONTENTS

GOD'S POETRY

Poetry has never been my top subject. Horace, Wordsworth, Poe and Frost would not be my first choice of afternoon company. There is, however, one poet I just can't get enough of.

He is the most passionate, over-the-top, romantic poet of time and eternity, who inscribes symphonic songs of burning love on the hearts of his beloved. His touch is personal, tender, and intimate—with a creativity, passion, uniqueness and inexpressible… expressivity that is nothing short of the greatest poetry.

He is the Lord.

His verses are all around us. The serenity of a swelling, warm, golden sun setting off the western coast of Italy into a calm, tired sea. The majestic view from the summit of the New Hampshire White Mountains as the vast blanket of ranges spreads out as far as the eye can see. The soft embrace of a gentle breeze; the harmonious hum of a forest stream. The joy one gets at an unexpected happy turn of events. The consolation of family. The prodigy of a delicate work of art or the awe of an imposing cathedral. The tender, gorgeous, brilliant complexity of a simple field flower. The mysterious otherworldliness of the voiceless deer. The silent and solemn flight of a bald eagle gliding over the pine islands of the Minnesota boundary waters. The comfort of a pet. Even a special meal. Everything is a whisper of love from God, his tender embrace. He is constantly whispering. Do we hear him?

He speaks our language. He embraces us in ways we understand—though not always. Sometimes it is an exciting embrace, joyful and motivating. Sometimes it is warm and consoling for our cold, fearful hearts. At other times, it means being pulled into his heart crowned with thorns. The closer we allow ourselves to be pulled in, the deeper we are pierced by those very thorns, and the more we become his intimates, not only in his joys, but also in his sorrows. But no matter what embraces we receive and when we receive them, they are embraces of infinite Love and Wisdom nonetheless. May we never forget.

His touch is unpredictable. "Sometimes, when the soul least thinks of it, and when it least desires it. [...] Sometimes, too, the divine touches are sudden, occurring even while the soul is occupied with something else. [...] They are also so sensible and efficacious, that at times they make not only the soul, but the body also, to tremble. At other times they come gently. [...] But they are not always equally sensible and efficacious, for they are very often exceedingly slight; but however slight they may be, one of these recollections and touches of God is more profitable to the soul than any other knowledge of, or meditation on, the creatures and works of God."[1] If only we knew the power of his touch. "For there are some [...] touches of God, wrought by him in the substance of the soul, which so enrich it that one of them is sufficient."[2]

Our life is a journey toward the eternal embrace of the Father. Joy, hope, pain and darkness are all part of the mystery and beauty of God's poetic style. He is the Divine

Poet, who is ever at our side, whispering his verses in our hearts to gently draw us into his arms.

The path is unique for each child because he loves each one personally. There is no cookie-cutter in the Divine Carpenter's workshop. "Along how many paths, in how many ways, by how many methods you show us love!"[3] He is constantly humming hymns in our ear. All that happens is loved or allowed by him to pull us into his arms. "Those who, in faith, entrust themselves to the guidance of the Holy Spirit come to realize how God is present and at work in every moment of our lives and history, patiently bringing to pass a history of salvation."[4]

Think how it must melt our Father's heart when we let him draw us into his arms. Give him this joy. "Behold this Heart which has so loved men that it has spared nothing, even to exhausting and consuming itself, in order to testify its love."[5] What a consolation for the Father when he can pull us in! Think about it. It is simple and beautiful. And this is life!

St Teresa of Avila and St John of the Cross have been two of the greatest reference points in my own journey. They have taught and inspired me so much. I consider them a big sister and brother. In their spiritual legacy, they trace out this journey towards "this most sweet touch and union […], the Divine Embracing."[6]

They describe it as the journey of the soul to its innermost dwelling places where he abides, passing through nights of purification in order to be fully emptied to receive him. This pilgrimage is strenuous and painful, yet inexpressibly beautiful and rewarding beyond compare because of the treasured embrace toward which we travel. Nothing on earth could compare to this fullness. The soul must take the first steps on the road with God's help, removing the obstacles that prevent Our Lord from drawing us into his heart. But very soon it reaches the stage when it can climb no higher by its own efforts. It then becomes God's work alone to pull the soul into his embrace.

But to say that we can do no more on our own is far from saying that the advance becomes slower. It is God's work, and thus it takes on his pace. The Father desires this embrace infinitely more than we do. We can't imagine what this desire means. He burns to pull us in and will do so if we let him. When he takes the reigns of the soul to lead it deeper into the interior castle… On his wings we fly! Teresa and John are able to transmit this experience in such a poignant way because they were docile and lived it firsthand. Their experiential wisdom has helped me tremendously in discerning the often confusing tunes that God has sung in my life.

Every day is filled with his gentle tugging at our hearts. He wants to lure us into himself with his poetry, but sometimes we don't notice him. We've experienced what it's like to show countless signs of love and receive no response in return as if we weren't even there. "We played the flute for you, but you did not dance, we sang a dirge but you did not mourn."[7] And God? We go through life so quickly that we don't notice these expressions of heart-rent love from him. We lose our sense of wonder. We fail to read his rhyme.

I wish I were more refined to appreciate all poetry. I look up to those who do. But may all of us at least learn to recognize those poems of love, those lullabies, that "silent music"[8] that he whispers to our hearts daily to draw us into his arms. He loves us so much, and he expresses it in every way he can. He burns for us! "I will lead her into the desert and speak to her heart."[9] "That where I am, you also may be!"[10] We often just don't have the sensitivity to perceive him. Life is beautiful, exciting, and adventurous, not because of what we do, but because we have a lover who seeks to win our hearts with his poetry. May we hear! May we love! May we respond with our own song!

The poems of this book are simple prayers of a son to his Father and his Beloved. They are a poetic response to his intimate, unrivaled poetry. There would be nothing powerful to sing of if it wasn't for the overwhelming power of his love. It is his work.

None of them were written to be heard except by the one to whom they are addressed. For this reason, there is no necessary linear flow of ideas between the poems nor professional perfection in their techniques. Each one is my best attempt to put into words one of his many poetic touches of Love in my life, experiences often so distant from each other in time and substance. Yet God's music is not random. There is always a hidden rhyme to his reason. I tried to identify these overtones of his song by dividing the poems into meditations in the context of a journey. He awakens (chapter 1) his children (chapter 2) to a journey home to him (chapter 3). This journey is filled with beauty and blessings (chapter 5), but also entails moments of confusion (chapter 4) and cross (chapter 6). Yet through it all, Our Lord never leaves our side (chapter 7) until we reach the journey's end, his unending embrace in Heaven (chapter 8). Each chapter begins with an initial reflection with many a wise word from St Teresa and St John of the Cross woven in for inspiration and guidance.

My hope is that in sharing these simple expressions of love, the reader will come to recognize that God's poetry fills his own life too. If he has touched this son so profoundly, how much more has he touched your heart? May this be an invitation in poor, unpolished words, to become like children, awing at the many poems of Love that embrace us daily. Each will hear it in his own way: whispers of love, epic poetry, a soft lullaby. He speaks to none of his children in the same way, but to all he speaks. Let him pull you into his embrace with his poetry. That is the only place you will find what you are really looking for. Feel his gentle touch, his warm embrace, his soothing voice pulling at your heart. It's there. You just have to listen. May we all learn to read his rhyme in our daily lives as he leads us along this journey home to his embrace.

Chapter 1

STINGING ARROW

How do you endure,
Oh life, not living where you live,
And being brought near death
By the arrows you receive
From that which you conceive of
Your Beloved?

Why, since you wounded
This heart, don't you heal it?
And why, since you stole it from me,
Do you leave it so,
And fail to carry off what you have stolen?[11]

† John of the Cross

God awakens us to our heaven-bound journey with his touch. He calls us home. "You made us for yourself, oh Lord, and our hearts are restless until they rest in you."[12] We were made for him, and for him we yearn, yet sin has cleaved us in two. This painful, bleeding chasm marks our entire journey to his embrace. "What I do, I do not understand. For I do not do what I want, but I do what I hate."[13]

So when God's beckoning touch penetrates so deeply into a heart so wounded, it is indescribably sweet, and yet unimaginably painful. "Oh living Flame of Love, that woundest tenderly my soul in its inmost depth! […] Oh sweet burn! Oh delicious wound! Oh tender hand! Oh gentle touch!"[14] "It seems this pain reaches to the soul's very depths, and that when he who wounds it draws out the arrow, it indeed seems, in accord with the deep love the soul feels, that God is drawing these very depths after him. […] This delightful pain—and it is not pain! […] The soul is left with the desire to suffer again that loving pain the spark causes."[15] We don't understand it. It is the pain of a thirst for that distant living water we have begun to taste on our parched lips.

But the Father is wise. "Thou hast wounded me, oh divine hand, that thou mayest heal me."[16] It is this very sting of Love by which he draws us on in the journey into his embrace. "Oh blessed wound inflicted by him who cannot but heal it!"[17] As we begin to perceive those faint murmurs of his melody in our ear, our hearts start to simmer and come alive. "When the gentle hunter wounded and subdued me, in love's arms, my soul fallen; new life receiving."[18]

This small flame begins to grow like the passion of two lovers. Soon we are consumed by this desire. "Your arrows have sunk deep in me."[19] And yet we still bear the scars of sin. We want to fly to God, but we are suffocated by the chains of wounds we don't rightly understand. And this kills us. We cry out to our beloved. Free us! We feel with St John of the Cross that he has stolen our heart, that he has struck us from afar with a consuming passion. But then he has run off, leaving us wounded in sin and yearning for him.[20] We run out into the streets like the bride of the Song of Songs. "Have you seen him whom my heart loves?"[21] But we cannot find him. A raging quest commences. He has pulled us out onto the road by this touch. The journey has begun.

This lover yearns for you. "God wants his bride!"[22] The Divine Archer has marked you. "The arrow he drew full of love."[23] He is beckoning you on this journey into his embrace. You aren't ready for home yet; you need the road to strengthen and purify you until there is no obstacle between you and him. Then he can pull you totally and unreservedly into that embrace for all eternity.

Awaken. Take up the road. He calls you on with his song!

SWEET DESERT

Aroma sweet draws on this dove
In swelling burn, with blade of Love,
Which pierces to the inner core
That from the dust with Lover soar.
To desert sweet in pain it leads.
With solitude and Cross it feeds.
A love that casts out all desire
But single love! Consuming fire!
Oh passion's Love, in you replete!
Alone with you in desert sweet!

COME INSTEAD TO ME

My Love, my Love, I long to fly
To desert, calm and still,
To drink from spring, with you alone,
This gaping chasm fill.

I long! I long for you, my Love.
This crying, bleeding fire,
Yet chains of iron banish far
This union I desire.

Wounding, weighing, choking chains,
Oh Love, I strain to break.
Robbing me of only need:
You, for whom I ache.

My Love, if I can't fly to you,
Bound in fearful cell,
Descend, my Love, descend to me.
Save me from this hell.

It doesn't matter where, my Love.
With you just let me be.
So, if I cannot come to you,
Then come instead to me.

FREEING FETTERS

Oh Lord, oh how I crave to soar
The heights of sonship in your arms,
Simple, free, my God adore,
Who never sweet Beloved harms.

Why to saints and not to me
This intimacy in you sustain,
While I, unwilling, graces flee,
Unwilling, grip my iron chain?

How long, oh Lord? Will I be free
To love thee as a simple son?
Free me, free me, let me be
Free to love, Beloved One.

And yet these fetters still may be
The link through which I cling to you.
Broken, humbled, come to thee
Without a boast or merit true.

Nothing in your arms to give,
Only in your arms to be,
As a son to simply live,
Eyes on you eternally.

Consuming Fire

Consuming flame, my heart can't bear!
O'erwhelming joy apart does tear.

Wordless, numbness, mystery.
Boundless love of God for me.

Too good! Beyond! I don't deserve
This bursting ocean, no reserve!

My Love, my Love, I... Here am I.
My whirling soul in ocean lie

In your embrace, that drowns in balm,
Unworldly peace, a raging calm.

A passion, burning, tranquil sigh,
A muted song of Lover nigh.

Too good! Too deep to yet be true.
Yet truest Love, Beloved! You!

PULL ME IN

A sweetest draw I can't resist,
Yet gentle, leaving me still free.
Unheeded oft', yet you persist
To whisper songs of love to me.
Why don't you weary, don't you leave
This stubborn child, this heart of stone?
No slight will break 'til you achieve
This son who leaves you oft' alone.
Oh tireless love, love undeserved,
Come free me; draw me in to you,
That faithful love spilled unreserved
May win this heart which you pursue.
You've sought this son eternally;
May this love pull me in to thee.

MY ONLY NEED

I can't continue on like this.
Admit I, God, you win.
Grinding, heaving 'gainst your will,
Exhausted, I give in.

Made for you, capricious strove
In other things console.
Not letting Father love his child,
Demanding full control.

Control I clasped and steered to fields
I proudly chose to feed,
Thinking I knew more than God
To quench my fashioned need.

But suffocation, I can't breathe.
Let off constricted heart.
What is going on in me,
Slowly torn apart?

This need, this need is killing me,
Which willingly I made.
Not Creator's need in me,
Whose plan I disobeyed.

Enough, enough, oh take away.
Free me, God, I see
The only need inscribed inside
Is in your arms to be.

Fashioned need, oh flee this heart,
Who made you yet does hate.
Ne'er meant to be this storm within
You needlessly create.

For though I do not know my heart,
And many harms concede,
The Father made and loves it more
And fills its only need.

How Long, My Love

I burn and strain for unearned gift,
Yet told by Love I still must wait.
Tormenting time sees us apart,
Yet ne'er delay this flame abate.

Delay, delay, this dull delay,
Which wrings my heart, my yearning heart.
Wait, oh wait, how long, my Love?
How long this time keep us apart?

I look, I reach, yet cannot grasp
A gift no merit could deserve.
Yet heart denies impossible
And burns on still without reserve.

Yet in this very waiting love
Does grow, and fervent flame is fanned
Still more; my hopes and heart's desire
By distance, waiting on, expand.

This separation, hidden gift,
Impels me on to strain for you.
My Love, I e'ermore burn, I yearn.
All tense with passion, you pursue.

Oh fruitful wait, which I can't change,
Oh time unmoved that tortures me,
I thank you for you love increase
'Til held in Love eternally.

LOST IN THE SEA OF LOVE

Wordless surge of clearest deep,
No desired longings keep,
But to stay, to look, to be
Immersed in sure uncharted sea.
Ne'er has, nor will a word be found
To voice where raging forces bound:
Emotion, feeling, sentiment,
Heart is torn and soul is rent.
O'erwhelmed by gentle, numbing breeze,
Where deep and piercing flames firm seize.
Not denied yet undescribed,
Sweet, yet bitter hum inscribed.
Clear yet undeciphered songs
To passion's Lover's heart belongs.
Unearned mystery from above:
Lost within a sea of Love.

REST

In frantic cares I long for rest,
Yet find it not in pain to flee,
But in your presence tranquil be,
And lay my head upon your chest.
Deceived by many mundane things,
Still drained e'en when I seek repose
In earthly joys I freely chose,
Yet no tranquility it brings.
My heart was made to rest in you,

And only here profounder joy
Than all life's pleasures could employ,
Ne'er achieving fullness true.
Restless 'til I rest in thee,
Where I'll rest eternally.

STINGING ARROW

This stinging arrow, barbed and sharp!
From where, who shot you at my heart?
You strike, you slay, yet I still live
In dark, cold valley, torn apart.

From where? Where hide you, drawing up?
Yet I sink down with heavy weight.
These chains of sin that suffocate,
That well a thirst I can't abate.

I strain in anguish, sigh! I die!
I look around. Oh where, my Love!
From where this arrow, burning cold,
This arrow shot from strings above!

I long to see, yet can't behold.
Oh where those sinews, where the bow?
Tormented by this sting of Love
That kills, from where I do not know.

Oh where, my Love, where do you hide?
From where this arrow, how I long!

I long to die, to sing, to dance,
Yet chained by sin, a muted song!

Oh free me, free me, let me fly
To precious archer seeking me.
Enough to hold, embrace and see.
Naught else I seek, with you to be.

Oh arrow shot from longed-for Dove,
Kill me; lead me to my Love.

Chapter 2

IDENTITY

I am yours and born for you;
What do you want of me? […]
Yours, you made me,
Yours, you saved me,
Yours, you endured me,
Yours, you called me,
Yours, you awaited me,
Yours, I did not stray.
What do you want of me?[24]

† Teresa of Avila

We are God's children. This is our identity, and this identity traces out our journey. He is our infinitely loving Father, who yearns in every way to draw us to his heart, the Father who receives his prodigal children home when we have squandered his treasures.[25] We are the beloved of the lover of the Song of Songs. "My Beloved is for me, and I am for my Beloved!"[26] He yearns for us. "He loves thee with liberality, without self-interest, only to do thee good, showing joyfully his countenance full of grace, and saying: I am thine and for thee, and it is my pleasure to be what I am, to give myself to thee and to be thine."[27] It's too good to be true.

"May today there be peace within. May you trust God that you are exactly where you are meant to be. [...] May you be content knowing you are a child of God. Let this presence settle into your bones, and allow your soul the freedom to sing, dance, praise and love. It is there for each and every one of us."[28] Our journey is sealed in sonship. Every element of it is chosen with personal Fatherly care from the one who knows best. There is no good he could give that he hasn't given. "The Lord is my shepherd. There is nothing I lack."[29] This should fill us with the greatest peace.

We don't need to understand everything. We are children. Peace. Trust. The Father's heart can't resist excessive trust, and this is the hallmark of a child. Someone who knows and loves more is leading. May we cling firmly to our identity as his children. May this unshakable and indelible truth shape our journey and give us the deepest peace.

Our worth doesn't come from the trail we blaze for ourselves, but from the path that has been handpicked by the hand that crafted us. We are who he made us to be, not what we make of ourselves. Who could add to the worth God has given us? We are his children. This is our glory. This is our identity.

IDENTITY

Oh heart that cries with gaping void,
So longing for a love to fill.
A pang in nature, ne'er to yield
'Til maker's balm a peace instill.

I seek approval undeserved,
Comparing, wanting to console,
Confirm myself in who I am,
Identity in my control.

Forcing others to affirm,
A role that ne'er was meant to be,
For not from them do I receive
Indelible security.

I am a son and nothing more,
Yet naught could ever add to this.
For who could fill a brimful vase,
Increasing joy to total bliss?

Naught to add, naught to take,
Unshaken for eternity,
Beloved son of Father dear,
This is my identity.

I BELONG TO YOU

I do the things that I abhor,
And you deserve from lover more,

Yet good and bad
Bouquet be had;
Receive it wilted, I implore.

Wilted, withered, still be blessed,
Though know not if it be my best.
I trust your grace,
Your warm embrace.
Accepted as I am, I rest.

Imperfect gift, no, less, it's true,
Inconstant childish gain pursue,
But, Love, behold,
And be consoled
By fact that I belong to you.

FATHER'S WISH

Let go, my son, and let me lead.
Your Father holds you in his arm.
Let go, I know your hidden need.
This pain you feel will cause no harm.

A perfect son I did not make,
Nor do I this demand of you.
Oh do not dread this for my sake.
A different diamond I pursue.

My love, I do not seek your skill,
Nor thousand gifts of value dear,

Nor that you, blameless, all fulfill,
Cow'ring, dreading, full of fear.

No, my son, it's simpler still,
For all I want is you to see,
A smiling child who trusts my will,
Who, tranquil, loving, rests in me.

Receive from me both good and bad,
Knowing all is tailored gift.
Confide in me your anguish sad,
Your joys unto my cheeks to lift.

A peaceful, happy, little one,
From Father's gaze to never part,
Open armed, a trusting son,
This the gift that melts my Heart.

Fear Not

Fear not, little child.
You're in God's embrace.
His arms wrap you round
With infinite grace.

Let go, foolish heart.
Oh how can you fear
When God holds you firm
To warming heart near.

Fear not, little one.
Your cares all release,
And sleep in his arms
In filial peace.

SELFLESS TEARS

Where are you, son? It's time to walk
Together in the breeze,
As always in the afternoon,
In shadow of the trees.

No answer came, for I did hide
In thicket out of fear,
For shame at filthy nakedness
When heard him drawing near.

What's wrong, my joy, my little one?
Oh no, my dear, my son!
Did you take of the fruit of death,
My loving counsel shun?

Speechless, shamed, I gazed in grief
Through thicket on his face,
And image saw what thousand years
Could ne'er from mind erase.

I saw a grief, so solemn, deep.
Those eyes! I cannot bear!
Those tear-filled eyes, oh Father dear,
My soul in two does tear.

Turn away, oh Father dear,
Those eyes of selfless tears.
They burn and slay this fallen child
In shame, in love, in fears.

I'd rather face a look of rage,
Of justice for my sin,
For pain of tearful selfless eyes
Consumes me from within.

But that is not my Father's heart.
Your own pain you see not.
But pain your child has caused himself,
Whom in your love begot.

Oh gaze of loving Father, may
These tears of selfless pain,
Shed for child who hurt himself,
Him back to you regain.

LOVE TO THE UNGRATEFUL

Why do you love this child so much?
Such warm and gentle care!
Why do you love this son so much?
Too good, I cannot bear!

This child that's ne'er done to deserve,
Such precious gazes win.
No! More! Ungrateful, seeking self,
Responds to love with sin.

Abusing, seeing as my own
This freely given grace.
Taking, leaving you alone,
Avoiding Lover's face.

And yet, oh Heart! You never cease
To freely, gently give
Your grace to this ungrateful son
As long as he should live.

Oh turn me, Love, to your sweet gaze,
This hardened heart renew.
For your sake open up my eyes,
These gifts draw me to you.

CHANNEL

A channel pure does not admit
Herself into entrusted stream.
No stone nor clay may she permit,
Lest she should sully native gleam;
For when she loses freshness clean,
She shows herself poor instrument.
Though fed from source's love pristine,
She through her load does self present.
So long as stream does not withhold
From further banks her crystal store,
Nor mix self with ambition bold
And tarnish what was chaste before,
Will life spring forth along her shore,
Which flows abundant evermore.

BAPTISMAL BEAUTY

Born into the life of God,
Share in Trinity,
Death to life, the Dove descends,
His living within thee.

One in immolation which
Christ does to Father lift,
Joined in Pasch of Worthy Lamb,
Pulled into the gift.

Washed in blood and water flowing
From his pierced side,
Child anew of pilgrim Church,
His body and his bride.

Oh beauty of this radiant soul,
Baptized in Mystery.
God dwells in you, the chains of death
Are shattered; you are free.

Refulgence bright, you blinding grace,
Who, knowing you, would dare
To sacrifice to death and vice
Your beauty pure and fair.

So high your God has lifted you,
Angelic dignity.
So much to lose, though, if you chose
To reach for passion's tree.

Cherish this pure radiance,
Integral and whole,
Gem unseen but no less real,
Almighty in your soul.

GLORY BE

If but one moment glory give
To my beloved loving King,
His undeserved graces sing,
Worth it to one moment live.
As flower who must simply be,
Without need else to say or do,
Just being as it's meant by you,
Giving glory silently.
So may his little children bring
No more than self to please their Lord.
No great astounding feats afford,
Nor virtues proudly triumphing.
Just simple song of sincere son
To Father, Son, and Spirit one.

GOD'S EMBRACE

Touch of God, so tender, soft,
Of Father, gentle, pure.
What could trouble little heart
In his embrace secure?

In finem[30] love, shown on the cross,
Wraps you, oh child, each day,
A love which holds your life secure,
A love you can't repay.

Peace then, oh child, for love unknown,
Which you can't see nor hear,
Nor touch, yet it envelops you,
Embrace of Father dear.

Chapter 3

JOURNEY

Do not be frightened, daughters, by the
many things you need to consider in order
to begin this divine journey which is the
royal road to Heaven. A great treasure is
gained by traveling this road.[31]

† Teresa of Avila

Our life is a journey. There is a path and a destination. We are not there yet, but are called to move forward, "living here as pilgrims, beggars, exiles, orphans, desolate wanderers, possessing nothing, and looking for everything above,"[32] "for we are at sea and journeying along this way."[33] All voyages are tiring, but we can't forget the home toward which we travel. Don't forget his embrace.

The road has its dark moments, its trials and confusion, but also the daylight, the beauty of the wayside and a companion for the way. There is fatigue and thirst, mountains to climb, tunnels to brave, valleys to bear, but these are not our goal. Our homeland is beyond. We are just passing through.

What a homeland awaits us, yet how often we lose sight. We take our eyes off Heaven as if earth were everything. Our life loses orientation and continues with the subconscious inertia of a direction we once had but lost. We lose hope and want to hang up our boots and climb no more. But we must keep walking. Don't give in to this lie of despair. "You must always proceed with this determination to die rather than fail to reach the end of the journey."[34]

"My home is in Heaven. I'm just traveling through this world."[35] This future homeland indelibly marks the present. "Christians, on pilgrimage toward the heavenly city, should seek and think of these things which are above. This duty in no way decreases, rather it increases the importance of their obligation to work with all men in the building of a more human world."[36]

No life on earth is perfect, but it doesn't have to be. We are on a journey. It doesn't end here. What peace this gives. There is something more waiting beyond the hills. One day we will be there.

JUST PASSING THROUGH

A man stepped off the train one day,
A man whom no one knew,
In light brown hat and simple suit,
A man just passing through.

Clean-cut and combed, with peaceful gait
And gentle, serene eye,
He went down to the station's court
To watch the passersby.

He sat alone upon a bench,
And pulled out from his vest
A precious worn-out paper scrap,
Kept safely at his chest.

And there he sat to watch them pass,
Each soul, a book of life.
Their faces, styles, and unknown joys,
Unknown their lot of strife.

A thousand looks, a thousand dreams,
A thousand thirsting hearts,
Waiting with no one to share
Until their train departs.

A thousand names unknown to him
Downcast did pass him by,
Journeying toward unknown home:
To where? For what? And why?

A thousand worlds under those eyes,
A hidden history
Of joy and pain, of loss and gain,
To him a mystery.

The fresh young widow, mourning still,
With tender child in hand.
The couple old who'd weathered time
And still together stand.

The slick, intent young businessman
Walks quickly unaware,
Busy with a thousand thoughts
As if no one were there.

The woman who parades herself
As object to be bought.
The man enslaved to substances,
Who shares the beggar's lot.

She walks and sips her coffee cup.
He yells into his phone.
She fears a man's malicious gaze
To wait 'til she's alone.

He holds her hand and gaily walks,
Just glad to have her near.
Another rushes through the crowd
With eyes that glare of fear.

The poor, the rich, the glad, the sad,
The empty, the content,

The sick, the strong, the worried one
Whom life's hard hand has bent.

He watched them all as they walked past,
Some with purpose clear:
A vivid goal, a destined end,
A home, a family dear.

For them the train was just a means,
Which homeward did them send.
A hope, a fire, which did inspire
Them to their journey's end.

Others passed with sunken eye.
He thought where would they go.
"I take the next train out of here.
To where, I do not know."

An endless, hopeless, joyless trek,
Drained of strength and drive,
With no one to support their pain;
They journey to survive.

Everyone would board a train.
One fact for all was true:
Regardless of their purpose, they
Were all just passing through.

Our man watched on as each soul passed,
Each universe, each book,
Each peaceful smile, serene with love,
Each anguished, empty look.

He wished they all could gaze erect,
That more than shoes may see
Of all those souls that they passed by,
Each one with silent plea.

Each with silent plea indeed,
Yet at the end of day,
Their journeys all would come to end,
And sleep drive woes away.

Then what of all the day's events,
While they the world did roam?
Whether it was their intent,
At last they'd all get home.

And when at home no difference makes
If pain was deep or not.
The struggles of that journey will
Forever be forgot.

So thought our man as he did watch
Each one his train pursue.
So different, yet each one of them
Was still just passing through.

At last the train's high whistle blew,
And "All Aboard," did sound.
The time had come for his train too.
He too was homeward bound.

He put away that faded scrap
Of paper in his vest,

An image of his wife just died,
Whom silently he missed and cried,
For she, his own life's warmest pride,
Had gone to ever rest.

He smiled and sighed and grabbed his bag
And donned his faded hat,
And walked out slowly from the court,
Where he had pensive sat.

And up the train he mounted with
A peace that's deep and true,
For each man's lot may rise and fall,
And journey's woes will him enthrall,
Yet in the end, it's worth it all
If we're just passing through.

SILENCE

In youthful years I drank the breeze,
A thirst I had to slate,
A quest, a void, a mystery mine,
That foam could not abate.

The urge did drive to loose the sails
And probe each varied sea
To find the place I could call home,
The waters made for me.

Rough and raging, cold and still,
Colorfully clear,

Each deep I tried yet ne'er did find
My place not far nor near.

At last I came home to the port
Where I set out at first,
Thinking that far off I'd find
Wherewith to fill this thirst.

Yet in that very haven calm
I found the answer clear.
All the while I searched without,
Yet all the while here.

I looked without, yet here within
My wild and searching heart,
Something, someone from whom I
Could not find peace apart.

For you were in me all along,
Though I did look abroad.
Silent guest, my comforter,
Gentle, loving God.

In silence comfort did I find,
And not at daring sea.
My Love united, calm and still,
His life inside of me.

HER JOURNEY HOME TO ME

Long before the sun was lit,
And all the stars above,
I dreamed about a little one,
Whom I would dearly love.

How beautiful my girl would be
Of body and of heart,
Made for Heaven e'er to be,
Ne'er from me to part.

Her life will be a constant quest,
So often hard to see,
But one day she will see it clear,
Her journey home to me.

I'll give her loving family;
I'll watch her thrive and grow,
And laugh and cry as she does try
My loving plan to know.

And when I know she's ready,
Her name to her I'll say.
I'll take her from that loving home,
And show to her the Way.

Then on that road she'll journey,
Long as it may be,
With tears of joy and pain and love,
Her journey home to me.

I'll catch her when she stumbles,
And find her when astray,
For in her love she'll truly seek
To know and walk my Way.

Sometimes she'll feel me present,
So near her to abide.
She'll see my hand in everything,
And know I'm at her side.

But sometimes I'll be hidden.
Conceal from her my face,
And she will feel that I am gone,
Though still in my embrace.

She'll ask me why I've left her,
And why I am not there.
This loneliness a burden cold,
So hard for her to bear.

My girl, I'll never leave you.
I'm here just as before,
And on my wings I'll raise you up
O'er mountains high to soar.

Hear my voice, my little one.
Listen, I will lead
With whispers soft and yet still clear.
I am all you need.

My little girl will make me proud.
She'll listen to my voice,

And give up all to follow me,
And make me her first choice.

And one day she'll have run the race,
And come unto the place,
Aided by my constant grace,
Home to my embrace.

And then she'll look back at the life,
And my plan she will see.
And understand the way I chose,
Her journey home to me.

Then she'll see the dots line up,
Which senseless did appear.
My loving plan at last she'll know,
Finally so clear.

No matter fog or storm or dark
That she will journey through,
Everything will be a gift
To prove her love is true.

For in that dark she'll call my name
When I seem far from her.
That loneliness which she will feel
Will make her love more pure.

No better plan could I have found
For my dear girl to go,
And when at last she's at my side
This wondrous truth she'll know.

And then she'll never leave my side,
With me eternally,
Having walked with faith and love
Her journey home to me.

WISDOM'S CARE

We didn't see those storm clouds brew,
Nor act when cold hail fell,
And winds arose and rocked our boat,
And ocean tides did swell.

So much that we had thought secure
At once now seemed as naught.
A searing fear took hold on deck,
And panic with it brought.

We wanted to abandon ship
And take to frantic flight,
With no one strong to lead us home,
To guide us through the fight.

We would have just disbanded there,
And dropped our ropes and gone.
But He held course on firm due north;
His wisdom guided on.

He led us on to haven safe,
To calm protected bay,

To shield our tattered weary ship
As winds and waves allay.

But why the need to journey through
Those menacing cold waves?
Why the need to, weak and torn,
Submit to him who saves?

Why not sail in pride and peace,
Not humbled by the strife?
Untouched, untested, shallowly
Enjoying easy life?

This wisdom makes no sense, it seems,
To make this proud ship bend,
Only then to bend himself
And gaping wounds attend.

Yet in his tending stronger makes
Her sails, her mast, her prow,
That even stronger winds may face
Than could she up to now.

Now healed and back to sea renewed,
Unfurled again her sail,
Stronger than had been before,
Reviving winds avail.

Unseen, unsought, yet in his love
He chose for us this sea,
To bring about a greater good
We ever thought could be.

So here we are and still we sail
With strength and love anew.
It wasn't us, but him alone,
Whose wisdom brought us through.

Unseen 'til Now

A field of flowers flanked the trail.
A painter's pallet varied bright,
Dancing in the smiling light
Of morning's gently rising veil.
Beauty's timely soothing balm
Healed my heart as I walked past.
A jar whose gift will ever last,
Ageless depths restoring calm.
This balm that girts this pleasant way,
Why did I ne'er see this gift?
My eyes from earth I ne'er did lift,
Though I did walk it every day.
Now raising eyes at last I see
The gifts this road e'er holds for me.

Chapter 4

LEAD ME BLIND

In darkness be my light.[37]

† Teresa of Avila

We are journeying towards his embrace like the disciples of Emmaus,[38] travelling on a road we don't fully understand. We began travelling by the light of day. We felt the call and saw the path, but the night set in, and sometimes even the stars that guided us through the chill of the dark disappear in the fog. "Why do you hide your face?"[39] We don't understand where God is leading or why he allows certain things to happen. His guiding touches were once so clear to the soul, and now "the light by which he could see them is taken away. Until it returns he doesn't see them, but not for that reason does he stop knowing they are present."[40] Christ is still at our side as he was with those disciples, even though "their eyes were prevented from seeing him."[41] And although the night has set in, we need to keep walking.

Children don't understand everything. We want to know and control, but we don't need to. The Father knows. A child can ask an explanation for everything, but he often wouldn't understand. At times the Father doesn't tell us in order to protect us, absorbing the pain in his own heart.

"As high as the heavens are above the earth, so are my ways above your ways and my thoughts above your thoughts."[42] We don't understand what God is trying to do in us. There is "no light […] from above, because Heaven seems shut and God hidden; [nor] from below."[43] Where are we going? Where is the next step? Are we supposed to take this step? So grave and yet so dark. We feel lost, and this is a pain that cuts much deeper than we can bear alone. "Surely darkness shall hide me, and night shall be my light."[44] It is dark, yes, but "darkness is not dark to you, and night shines as the day. Darkness and light are but one."[45]

It is like hiking a mountain in the fog. You can't see where the path leads. All you can see is the next marker. You climb from marker to marker, trusting him who placed them there. He knows the way. We don't always see where God is leading us. We travel "in the darkness, but with the certainty that God keeps his promises."[46] His plan is obscure. Certain events in life, most especially the painful ones, seem to be left unexplained by our loving Father. Yet wouldn't it be foolish to distrust the trail markers in the fog? "I do not ask to see the distant hill. One step enough for me."[47] Maybe the path twists and turns and leads up steep slopes, but the fog prevents us from seeing the chasms, drop-offs, dead ends, deviations and dangers the path is avoiding. We can only trust our guide.

St Teresa narrates her life experiences and her understanding of the spiritual life with disarming sincerity. She often admits she doesn't understand. "I don't understand why this is; and that I don't understand gives me great delight."[48] He knows even if I don't. John describes the journey to God as traveling through the night so that we no longer trust ourselves but him. He will guide us in the dark. "It is therefore a singular grace from God when he so darkens and impoverishes the soul as to leave in it nothing which can lead it astray."[49] God allows this darkness and inability to understand in order that we have "nothing to do but to walk in the beaten path, [...] looking for all its blessings in Heaven; living here as pilgrims, beggars, exiles, orphans, desolate wanderers, possessing nothing, and looking for everything above."[50]

Do not be afraid. It will be dark, yes. This darkness will painfully pierce us to the very core, yes. We will cry out, yes. But trust him who knows. "Let nothing trouble you; let nothing scare you. All is fleeting. God alone is unchanging. Patience everything obtains. Whoever possesses God nothing wants. God alone suffices."[51]

We need to learn to travel through the night.

LEAD ME BLIND

Do you still speak?
Where now that voice
That once did talk in tone
So quiet, yet
Consoling me
When I felt cold, alone?

When I had doubts,
I'd turn my gaze
To you, and you would fill
My soul with peace
To know you here,
Defending from this chill.

Now have you ceased
To speak to me?
Or have my ears been closed?
For I hear not
Those guiding words,
Which way of Truth exposed.

Too much? Too fast?
Too little? Slow?
Where? How can I know,
If muted voice
Of guide unheard,
If you the way don't show?

If I can't see
The road ahead,

Nor guiding star may find,
May I still walk
My homeward trek.
My Guide, now lead me blind!

WHY THIS ROAD

Why these alleys, towering, slim,
Humid, stifling view of end,
Mucky streets, depressing dim?
Why such paths do you intend?

Why these weedy, unkept paths,
Thorny, left in disarray?
Why not reasoned road pursue?
Why for me this winding way?

Why for others charted road
That easy, sure ahead may go?
They know their times, their turns, their route.
Mine uncertain. I don't know.

"Hush this cry. My love unique.
For each I choose the way that's best.
I looked on you and found this path
To lead you to my soothing rest.

"My son, it's better not to see
This loving journey home to me.
I'll lead you. Trust, that you may be
In my embrace eternally."

Let God Lead

Peace, my soul, and let God lead.
Panic not, although you bleed.
Let him sculpt; let him heal
Through the anguish you now feel.
In verdant pastures he will feed.
Peace, my soul, and let God lead.

All Will Be Okay

Lord!
I don't know what to ask.
Lord!
What do I say?
Lord!
I can't go on like this.
Lord!
Make it okay!

I do not even know my need.
Lord!
How can I pray?
You know this pain; you know the cure.
Lord!
Make it okay!

I trust you, Lord; you know the way.
Lead!
I will obey.
Abandoned blind to your embrace,
All will be okay.

HIDDEN STAR

Light! Is this my precious star,
Which set me on this journey far,
But soon behind the hills did hide
And cease this pilgrim on to guide?
I see again; renew this heart,
Yet feel I you will soon depart.
Just ne'er let me forget the Way
You pointed on that parting day.
When I can see and when you're gone,
Teach me, Light, to journey on.

UNKNOWN FEAR

My cross, what will you ask of me?
I fear. I do not know.
Uncertain. Doubt. I cannot see.
Oh please, your secrets show.

My fainting heart, so frail, so small!
Please tell me where you lead.
Silent. You don't speak at all.
Unheeded, on I bleed.

Too heavy for my strength to bear?
Too sharp your splintered side?
My heart is stifled! Heavy care!
Knows not the pains you hide!

Knowing not your pains indeed,
Yet somehow for my good,
For Giver ne'er to harm would lead.
Then sweet must be your wood.

My bitter load, I fear you still,
Yet know you must be sweet,
For certain it is Giver's will
My joy to be complete.

GOD'S TIME

My Lord, my Lord, how slow the pace,
This humid, heavy, heaving march
Of time that fails my thirst to slate
And dry my hope, my body parch.

Oh time, how slow, I cannot wait.
I want control; I want it now.
The future dark, unseen, unknown,
Yet now I want, though know not how.

An unknown distant food I seek,
For now this repast fills me not.
I do not lie in loving arms
Of Father, who this son begot.

As though he knew not what I need,
This moment now to joyous live.
This son who wants to see and choose
And not let Father freely give.

As if he didn't want my good,
To satisfy the throbbing wish
Of son, this yearning e'er for more,
Impose a scorpion for a fish.

Now, oh now, I cannot wait
To see if you will care for me.
I want the feast. I want it now.
I want control. I want to see.

Hush, my soul, the Father loves.
Wait and trust. He better knows
The time and place his gift to give
By which unfailing love he shows.

My Love, I loose this frantic grip,
This need the future to control.
Surrender to a wiser care,
Where greener pastures will console.

Fog

Set out, known not from when or where,
On unknown road, if rough or fair,
Through unknown straits with unknown rests,
Unknown valleys, unknown crests.
A fog around, and all I see
Just one more step in front of me.
Yet one more step is all I need,
For wiser hand does, loving, lead.

UNKNOWN WAY

I do not ask.
I do not know.
I don't demand
Your ways to show.
As long as you
Are at my side,
And take my hand,
And blindly guide.
Although my heart
May tensely bleed,
I trust in you
To homeward lead.

NORTH STAR

I wandered through the plain at night
With dark sky overhead,
And chilling breeze and howling calm
Did slay that ground I tread.

A thousand torches danced above,
Yet one star only proved
To stand its ground while all else turned,
As Heaven's ocean moved.

Yet I, seduced by swirling stars,
From homeland turned away.

Though firm fixed guide did constant point,
I chose to walk astray.

Those whirling lights did mesmerize
This burning, panting heart,
And blinded by their glitter cheap,
Did tear this heart apart.

But now their shifting emptiness,
Which fooled me from afar,
Has filled me with devouring thirst
To find that stable star.

Oh where that star among this host,
Who leads to light of day?
Oh come, my Light, my true North Star,
Show again the Way!

Chapter 5

GIFTS OF THE WAYSIDE

May he be blessed forever who grants so many favors to one who responds so poorly to gifts as great as these.[52]

† Teresa of Avila

Often we complain "why me"; but do we know how to wonder "why me" in humble gratitude for the countless undeserved blessings that fill our journey? "If you knew the gift of God!"[53] Why me? Why did he create me with love from all eternity? Why did he come as a little baby in Bethlehem for me? Why did he die on the cross for me? Why does he choose to stay with me in the Eucharist? Why has God loved me so much throughout my whole life? We lose our sense of wonder and gratitude at the sacred gifts that surround us undeserved.

Life is filled with gifts: God's gifts and the gift of God himself. We don't deserve them, and we often don't respond. Why are you so good, Lord? Do you really know the weakness of this little one you are so blessing? "Lord, look what you are doing. Don't forget so quickly my great wickedness. Now that in order to pardon me you have forgotten it, I beseech you to remember it that you might put a limit on your favors. Don't, my Creator, pour such precious liqueur in so broken a bottle; you have already seen at other times how I only spill and waste it. Don't place a treasure like this in a place where cupidity for life's consolations is still not cast off as it should be; otherwise it will be badly squandered. How is it that you surrender the strength of this city and the keys to its fortress to so cowardly a mayor who at the first attack allows the enemy to enter? Don't let your love be so great, eternal King, as to place in risk such precious jewels."[54]

He didn't have to give these gifts, but he did. It didn't have to be this way, but it is. May we become like children again, and regain our appreciation and wonder for the many signs of his love. May our heart be "wounded with love of that beauty of the Beloved which it traces in created things."[55] The Incarnation, Christ coming down to console me at my side! The Eucharist! God's goodness painted in the creatures around me, "clothed with admirable beauty, and supernatural virtue derived from the infinite supernatural beauty of the face of God!"[56] "The grace, wisdom, and loveliness which flow from God over all created things!"[57] All the little unperceived gifts that flood my day with his subtle love! It's overwhelming! And all this to show his love for me.

How different life would be if we lived with grateful wonder rather than complaining for the few things we think we deserve. May we not walk this journey as sullen pilgrims. Yes, we journey through a valley of tears, but our Father wants to dry those tears with his love and company. May we not be blind to his gifts, but open our eyes to behold this poetic paternal beauty all around us.

LOOK BEYOND

A silent, beaming testament
Of something just behind,
Beauty blankets earth and sky
That something more may find.

Dilated sun in glowing orange
Sets gently in the deep
With tranquil, turquoise, timid waves,
Another eve to sleep.

Blue bashful orchid spreads her arms
In fragile symmetry.
Soft, unthreatening whirl of life,
Immobile majesty.

O'er reigning mountain peers the moon,
A rising blood-orange crest,
Announcing calm to fierce and frail,
To contemplate and rest.

The sparkling brook that gently hums
Refreshes solemn deer,
And singing birds in canopy
Harmonious appear.

A starry sky imposing shines
With brilliance from the past,
Telling wonders far beyond
Our world, a cosmos vast.

Singing, whispering, sparkling, soft,
Brilliant, beaming bright,
Raging, running, standing still,
Silent solemn sight.

Nature's beauty blows the bounds
Of what mind can define,
And oft' it sees, cannot but say
It is itself divine.

But deeper gaze, it all points up.
Look close and you will find
This beauty pure ends not in self.
There's someone's hand behind.

PRICELESS GIFT

Most costly gifts poured out in me,
Bought with my Beloved's blood,
Freely given, undeserved,
Gushing river, ceaseless flood.

You paid so dearly on the cross
To give your precious gems to me,
And effortless do I receive
Such costly, finest jewels free.

It shames me, Love, that you should pay
The price that rightly is my due.

You take my place, my ransom pay.
My sinful debt falls crushing you.

The shame, yet least that I can do,
With spirit humble, grateful, mild,
Receive these gifts from gentle hand,
Bought by Lover for his child.

It isn't just that I should have
Such treasures freely from above,
Yet you have paid the highest price
To priceless give this child you love.

Unfathomed Gift

A ne'er breached void,
A ship lost adrift,
Unheard of, confounding,
Oh unfathomed gift.

So helpless this ship,
A child in the snow,
Yet unfathomed gift
Descending so low.

Not wanting, unknowing,
Ungrateful as stone.
Thus unseen, unwanted,
He comes to his own.

Our God becomes man;
Man beholds God.
Oh unfathomed gift,
At our side to trod.

Thank you, Lord, thank you,
You unfathomed gift,
You, who to man come,
Thus man to God lift.

You take on our weakness,
Our throbbing, our tears,
The tempest inside us,
The pangs of the years.

The heat of our passion,
Scorchingly hot,
The chill of our darkness
In cold corners wrought.

Unfathomed by gentiles
Who do not believe,
Who flesh as an evil,
As weakness conceive.

But not our Creator,
For through flesh he shows
His love for his children,
Whose weakness he knows.

How noble this flesh, then,
Which God did assume,

And walk with his children
In valley of gloom.

Yet nobler still,
For when Son did rise,
He took back his body,
Eternal to prize.

Not just for a lifetime,
Nor ages untold.
Eternally wanting
His human flesh hold.

Eternally with us,
With nothing divide.
At his side forever
With Father abide.

Oh wonder in flesh,
Which heals sinful rift!
Oh God become man,
Oh unfathomed gift!

OH EMMANUEL

Emmanuel, Emmanuel,
Oh who conceive such untold love!
Emmanuel, you with us dwell.
Stay not apart in throne above.
Breaching gap we could not cross,

Unworthy we, who merit not,
Yet you, in love, take up our loss
And coming down, this gift rebought.
Emmanuel, Emmanuel,
What gift of love: you with us dwell.

WHY THEN

Why when census stirred the land,
The first in many years,
When mother had to leave her home,
This little child appears?

Why in winter; why at night
When there's no room at inns,
And in a trough, Our God on High
His earthly trek begins?

Why when king would seek his life,
And many die instead,
And far away to strange land flee,
'Til he who sought was dead?

Why then, why there in normal life,
Unseen you chose to trod?
Your ways are not the ways of men:
The loving ways of God.

Undeserved Redemption

You didn't have to choose this road,
Unnecessary gift.
When wounded, fallen child did run,
Yet back to Father lift.

You made him to enjoy your life,
And with his Father talk,
And through the breeze and cool of eve,
In garden with him walk.

Yet from such love he turned his gaze
And saw that cloying tree.
Forgot your gift, your word, your care.
To fatal fruit did flee.

He stretched his hand and took that fruit,
From your arms turned away.
Incurred for self eternal grief,
A debt he ne'er could pay.

You could have let him face his crime
And die in filth of sin,
But you did choose to bring him back
To your embrace again.

Yet still you'd every right to choose
An easy, costless way
To bring this rebel son back home,
His shameless sin repay.

Enough to merely will this cure,
Desiring from afar,
And he would stand as did before,
Freed from blackened scar.

Beyond yet still, for you did choose
Yourself to take the blame:
A fearful, anguished, horrid price
To take away our shame.

Oh thank you, Jesus, bursting Heart.
It didn't have to be.
Mysterious love, above, beyond,
Your Passion pure for me.

I'll never know just what it means,
This Love that carried through
Such undeserved redemptive work
To bring me back to you.

THE WHIRLWIND

A burning whirlwind of desire
To share with us th' eternal meal,
Yet full aware what would transpire,
The agony within conceal.

A yearning to complete the race,
Establish firm the heavenly reign,
Yet price to bring this rule of grace,
A fear that pulses every vein.

Oh Passion! How that ardent heart,
Drowned deep within a lonely sea,
Must ache inside so torn apart
With flaming longings contrary.

This heart in violent tempest thrown,
Leaves, that the wand'ring flock may eat,
His body, blood, his very own,
Poured out in full, his gift complete.

What precious, final, longed-for gift,
The gift of Passion from above,
This bread and wine, to Heaven lift,
Unending song of wordless Love.

GIFT OF GOLD

A harmony,
A note that strikes
A chord within the heart.

A resonance,
A oneness felt,
That joins to one each part.

A gift of gold
In earthenware
God does to us impart.

The Stream

A distant stream of golden light
Through darkened void begins to flow:
Creation's birth now pierces dark,
And we begin his Love to know.

Into this void this stream gives breath,
Though starting as a trickling rill.
New life springs up upon its banks,
And ocean's deep begins to fill.

The human fam'ly grows and thrives,
Yet drowned in selfish ways, begins
To look at fruits and not to God
And turn to crude and horrid sins.

The stream now grows; Creator shows
His Father's love as strong and stern.
Through flood and plague and quail and wars,
A just and jealous God we learn.

And revelation's constant stream
Makes ocean's tide to rise and swell
With judges, prophets, priests and kings,
This ocean deep of God's love tell.

And when time's fullness comes at last,
Now here Emmanuel may see,
God with us, whom we could touch,
The day of his Epiphany.

He walked with us, proclaiming Love,
This ocean, to his final breath:
His Passion, sacrifice, and tomb,
And rising still to conquer death.

This raging river, seething stream,
No dull indifference to such pull,
Nor ocean's arms to cradle more:
Our God reveals himself in full.

Fullness bright of Time itself,
Aft' centuries has burst at last,
But know you God, and know his Love:
This fullness not a tale of past.

For though the sea can hold no more,
The stream flows on with violent pace,
And ocean's shores now overflow
With waters of redemptive grace.

He couldn't bear to see this stream
Remain of old, event in chains,
So God gave us this Mystery,
Which fullness of this sea maintains.

For silent in the Eucharist,
Preserves for all until time's end
The full revealing of himself:
Creation 'til from earth ascend.

Oh miracle! Oh mystery!
What awe that we below may keep

The fullness of God's love with us,
This flowing stream, this ocean deep.

IRRESISTIBLE

Can coals within a furnace hot
Refuse to brightly glow?
Or cold debris in river tossed
Not with that river flow?

Can stones within a flowerbed
Not share the rose's scent?
Or leafy boughs 'neath early snow
Remain unmoved, unbent?

Can water not be turned to ice
Amid the freezing cold?
Or when some danger threatens child,
Can father not be bold?

Can ship sail calm across the sea
When rages violent storm?
Or lovers look indifferently
On feelings deep and warm?

When autumn frost is setting in,
Can leaves remain unturned?
Or thrown into a blazing fire,
Can wood remain unburned?

Could Moses stand before his God
And still leave not a trace?
For each time he before him stood,
They covered up his face.

And we, who, in the Eucharist,
To holy ground here came,
Can we now leave this sacred place
And go back home the same?

So Much More

Heart of God, you eager well,
For more than come to earth,
More than share our face and pain
Intended by your birth.

More than teach by word and deed
A truth as yet untold.
More than die and conquer Hell
To ransom back your fold.

Comprehension cannot grasp
The gift you came to give:
Communion with the Trinity,
That one with God may live.

Beyond what man could ever dream,
This helpless infant's goal.
The Triune God in us abides,
His presence in our soul.

Untold by God, unseen by man,
This gift is so much more!
Communion with the Trinity,
Whom earth and Heav'n adore.

INFINITE MERCY

Infinite? Can it be true?
Does boundless mercy me pursue?
Lost and hopeless, heart would say,
Yet it can't fathom mercy's way.
Tireless, though I tire to seek.
Repeated failure, jealous, weak.
Denying boundless love exists,
Yet in denial, it persists.
Justice of another kind,
To repeated buffets blind.
Price must pay, yet not by thief;
By mercy's blood is bought relief.
Too good, it can't, it cannot be,
This endless river flowing free.
Some limit, yes, to crystal well.
No, endless is its sweetened swell.
Try not to capture nor to know,
But in your soul let grateful flow.
None can merit, though he try.
None demand, none can buy.
Too good, this Mercy, to be true,
Bought by blood of Love for you.

Chapter 6

DARK VALLEYS

The trials suffered were well worth it.[58]

† Teresa of Avila

Suffering is the rhyme scheme of God's poetry. "Whoever wishes to come after me must deny himself, take up his cross and follow me."[59] The cross is an inevitable yet beautiful part of this journey to his embrace. "It alone is the road leading to Heaven."[60]

We know that there is no life without crosses, and yet in the moment of trial, we think it's unfair. We are always grappling with the mystery of our sufferings. "How can this possibly be for my good? How could a loving Father allow this?" When we think we understand it, a new twist sends us spiraling into confusion again. Yet Christ himself chose to be weak and to suffer. "Now then, if His Majesty says that the divine and sinless flesh is weak, how is it we desire our flesh to be so strong that it doesn't feel the persecutions and the trials that can come to it?"[61] The cross is part of being children of the Father.

St Faustina says that the angels are jealous of us because we can suffer for God.[62] The cross is a gift. "Well, see here, daughters," St Teresa says, "what he [the Father] gave to the one he loved most [the Son]? […] For these are his gifts in this world. […] He will see that whoever loves him much will be able to suffer much for him."[63] God blesses those he loves with sufferings and difficulties because it is through them that he draws us to himself. "It was good for me to be afflicted, in order to learn your laws."[64]

Suffering makes us more like the Beloved. We can't call ourselves lovers of the "Man of Suffering"[65] if we reject trials. "I would always choose the path of suffering, if only to imitate our Lord Jesus Christ if there were no other gain; especially, since there are always so many other benefits."[66]

Suffering purifies and proves us. "For in fire gold is tested."[67] "Iron cannot be fashioned according to the pattern of the artificer but through the instrumentality of fire and the hammer."[68] "The Lord often desires to give these torments and the many other temptations that occur in order to try his lovers and know whether they will be able to drink the chalice and help him carry the cross before he lays great treasures within them."[69] Trials are flames that purify our hearts and free us from what prevents us from flying into his arms. They liberate us to love. "Captive is he that loves you not," Teresa tells the cross. "No freedom does he know."[70]

Our Lord knows what we can bear and what is best for us. "Thou hast wounded me, oh divine hand, that thou mayest heal me."[71] We need to believe this. He only allows us to suffer because he sees the precious gain we can garner through suffering and in no other way. "All these sufferings are meant to increase one's desire to enjoy the Spouse."[72] Trials are anxious overflows of love from the Father's heart to pull us into his arms. Because of this, Teresa says, "I would not exchange those trials for all the world's treasures."[73] "For the increase of love of God I saw in my soul and many other things reached such a point that I was amazed; and this makes me unable to stop desiring trials."[74] "Give me trials, Lord," she exclaims. "Give me persecutions."[75] She said the souls who experience the beauty that comes from these pains are "like soldiers who are happier when there are more wars because they then hope to earn more."[76] "God, in fact, never permits any loss to come to a person truly mortified save for a greater gain."[77] "The greater the opposition the greater the gain."[78]

There will be moments where the dark chill of a lonely pain pierces so deep that our hearts bleed in anguish. But when touched by suffering, may we see the tender touch of God. May our heart recognize "the great gain and progress that comes to it by suffering for God."[79]

Embrace these gifts. The time to do so is short. May we not arrive to eternity, where "he will wipe every tear from their eyes, and there shall be no more death or mourning, wailing or pain,"[80] with the one regret that we didn't cherish those few moments that we had, infinitely short in the face of eternity, to love and grow through suffering.

"So, let's not complain of fears or become discouraged at seeing our nature weak and without strength. Let us strive to strengthen ourselves with humility and understand clearly the little we ourselves can do and that if God does not favor us, we are nothing. Let us distrust completely our own strength and confide in his mercy."[81] Trust him. Embrace this gift, which we will never fully understand. We don't need to. Trials are mysterious, incomprehensible, and precious. We will understand better from the other side. They are outbursts of the Father's heart to pull us into himself.

THE ICEBREAKER

There was a time when ship did glide
As weightless through the sea,
And sails did swell with ocean's tide,
Which stead'ly carried me.

But now my soul is numb and sore,
The jar of oil gone dry.
The free winds don't impel me more.
My sails now empty fly.

Though faithful to this day they've sped,
They can lead on no more,
For icy desert lies ahead
'Twixt me and destined shore.

And driven by the tide alone,
I can't reach northern peak.
A stronger force than sails windblown
To reach that which I seek.

The strength to pierce the biting cold
And miles of ice cut through,
That I the goal at last behold,
Which I through all pursue.

Where this strength? My need! Oh where?
Which cuts through ice and foam?
Oh come, deep Love, my ship now bear
Unto its final home.

THE WELL

Trapped deep down in prison well.
Piercing chill of clammy cold.
Dark, with no light to behold
Way to flee this fearful hell.
Constricting stones of putrid slime
Steal away all human hope.
Where my ladder, chain, or rope?
To freedom's air a futile climb!
Heart beats low of nightmare's fear,
Longing in this lonely place
For some sign of saving grace,
Searching for redemption near.
But, wait, I sense some gaze above,
Watching over me with love.

ADVANCELESS GAIN

A war that strains from morn to night.
How tense the fibers, bleeding heart!
A constant strife within it fight
Of mind and flesh and will apart.

The thorn inside, the constant prick,
The urge to counter chosen way.
Exhaust, fatigue and fever sick,
The irony within us play.

Unending wage with no restrain,
Unconquered flesh leaves no relief.

The constant push, the unseen gain,
This paradox in realm of grief.

Oh waging war in depths of me,
What meaning can you pointless give?
No victory 'ere sunset see;
Advanceless strife each day I live.

The storm, the flame, the wind, the hail,
The grind of time, mysterious blows!
A helpless ship with tattered sail,
In darkened sea adrift it goes.

Twisted, tangled, torn in two,
Distended by opposing force!
How long, oh Lord, must I pursue
The anguish of this great divorce.

Yet o'er the valley shines a Light!
Now comes to me th' Eternal One.
His glory now revealed to sight
As Father's own begotten Son.

This brilliant burst here beaming bright
Descends, with fallen man abide
In flesh and blood, in touch and sight,
To share this strife, warm at my side.

You chose to sanctify this strife
That flogs me from my infant days,
To teach the gift of such a life,
That mine are not Creator's ways.

Fear not this rift of flesh and soul,
The earthly fruit of human sin.
One day will dawn when reached our goal,
Ever healed, our rest begin.

Though earthly strife will ne'er alight,
With small advance, yet no small gain,
Our Mediator blessed this fight
By sharing in his children's pain.

CAN'T GO ON

I can't go on.
The pain too deep;
The drain too long.

To right, to left,
No word compose
My empty song.

The valley dry
With empty wells.
No more pursue.

I can't go on.
My only strength
Is come to you.

Numbed Soul

My soul feels numbed.
The drive I used to have
No longer impels me blindly.

Running through life
Without a chance
To look where I was going.

Watch your step!
Where your drive?
The jug is parched and dry.

But 'round I look,
And you are still here!
Your rod and your staff to comfort.

What is it all?
What has some worth?
What at the end of day?

Feelings cease!
Love takes over!
Frenzy, fury, gone.

Love takes over!
Lead me on!
Sure, secure, and faithful.

Slow and steady,
The ship embarks.
Prepares for icy seas.

The captain knows.
Stick to course.
He faithful leads me on.

Take Away

Take away, My Love, I beg,
These binding, strangling chains
That suffocate my yearning heart
In willed, unwanted pains.

They tear me from the only thing
My heart seeks to embrace:
To be embraced by you, My Love,
No longer shadows chase.

I push away most tender love
That seeks to draw me in,
Yet it the key to set me free
From chilling chains of sin.

Oh free me, Love, oh take away
These chasms I pursue,
And let me rest as child set free,
Poor, yet rich in you.

Slippery Slope

A longed-for height, above, beyond.
I gaze, I long, I seek.

I heave and strain and groan and grind,
Yet ne'er approach the peak.

My God, my God, in filth I lie,
And, blind, I helpless grope.
I dig my nails deep in mud
To scale this slippery slope.

And every little gain I make,
I slide back down deceived.
Despairing I could ever reach
The heights I once believed.

Oh, help me, Love, I gasp and cry
At bottom of this slope,
In filth and shame that pierces cold
And darkens infant hope.

I reach to you this sullied hand,
Which once was young and strong.
Now prematurely aged and pale,
Redemption's grasp does long.

And as before, on troubled sea,
You grasped at desperate call,
This dirty hand which stretches high,
Will not unanswered fall.

Chapter 7

COMPANION

What greater good could I want in this life than to be so close to you, that there be no division between you and me? With this companionship, what can be difficult? What can one not undertake for you, being so closely joined?[82]

† Teresa of Avila

This journey to the embrace of the Father would be unbearably lonely if we had to travel it in solitude. Very often we feel isolated. With the disciples on their way to Emmaus, we cry out from the depths of a cold heart: "Stay with us."[83] We yearn for an intimate companion.

"I am with you always."[84]

So "let nothing trouble you; let nothing scare you."[85] "Even when I walk through a dark valley, I fear no harm, for you are at my side."[86] He will never leave us.

It didn't have to be this way. He didn't have to come down as man to live alongside us as our companion. He didn't have to stay in our hearts through baptism and on our altars through the Eucharist. It could have been some other way. This is Divine Love: a tender love that never wants us to suffer without the comfort of knowing we are in his arms!

And just as we need the embrace of a friend much more when most crushed, when we have lost what is most precious or are at our breaking point, so may we always feel him at our side, especially when we are broken. He is always closer than it feels. He chooses to be, even though we don't appreciate the depths of such tenderness. What a humble, loving God! May we never cease to wonder at this love, which is so omnipotent and yet so gentle and close.

Christ is always there for us and knows what we go through. There is no trial we will ever have to bear that he has not borne first. "For we do not have a high priest who is unable to sympathize with our weaknesses, but one who has similarly been tested in every way."[87] He feels the same pain we do on this path. "Yet it was our infirmities that he bore, our sufferings that he endured."[88] This inspired Teresa to say, "There is no trial that it wasn't good for me to suffer once I looked at you as you were standing before the judges. Whoever lives in the presence of so good a friend and excellent a leader, who went ahead of us to be the first to suffer, can endure all things."[89] "Pay no attention to sufferings that come to an end if through them some greater service is rendered to him who endured so many for us."[90] Jesus isn't just there at our side. He is there, and he suffers with us.

When the storms of life rage and we begin to sink, when loneliness and isolation sever any courage to carry on, he comes to us on the waters of our life, reaches out, takes our hand, and pulls us up.[91] Let him sustain you. He yearns to. He will walk at your side and share your pain. In the comfort of his company, we will find the strength to journey on.

ONLY HIM

Rumbling tremor,
Roar of raging wind,
Fill my soul with fear.
Hush, my soul.
Only Him.
Jesus with you here.

Future, worries,
Racing through my mind,
Things I can't control.
Hush, my soul.
Only Him.
He your heart console.

Envy, others,
Wanting to compare,
Tear my soul apart.
Hush, my soul.
Only Him.
He will fill your heart.

Good and holy
Things I want to do,
Yet will e'er come true?
Hush, my soul.
Only Him.
He will carry through.

Thousand cares
Formless block my view,
Cause my heart to bleed.

Hush, my soul.
Only Him.
He is all you need.

MY BURNING NEED

Come, my Jesus, hurry here.
My soul moans in the night.
You, the Truth for which I yearn,
Come to bring your light.

You didn't have to come to save,
Yet come you did indeed
To melt my heart with infant eyes,
From cold despair to lead.

Though you gain naught by reaching down,
You lovingly extend
Your baby hand and silent say,
"Your chains at last will end."

And soul is filled with brilliance bright,
For ransom now is here.
My burning need has come to me,
My hope so small, so near.

SOLE DESIRE

You came with nothing, wanting not,
Content with manger cold,

Yearning only for my heart
In little hands to hold.

How much I mean to tender God,
Who burns with only care
To be with me, to join my song,
This melody to share.

If I was not enough for you,
Else you would have chose
Than chilling stall and bed of straw
For newborn to repose.

Oh may my heart be free for you,
This richest poverty.
My greatest joy in you, my Love,
As you are all for me.

OPEN GAZE

Serene and slow, surrendered soul,
As tender, tranquil dove,
Open wide to thus receive
Those thirsting wounds of love.

Vulnerable, your outward look,
Welcoming the need
Of flock without a shepherd sure,
Unknowing hunger feed.

No rigid track, unbending course,
Nor thickened barriers raise,

But open heart, receiving arms,
Your gentle, loving gaze.

COME OFF THE CROSS

"Come down, come down, come off the cross,
And then I will believe."
I can't, dear child, for from this throne
Your burden I relieve.

My child, my love, in spite of all
The harm you do to me,
The spit, the blows, the rods, the chains,
I will not quit this tree.

You mock and jeer, my love, yet I
Will love you to the end.
I will not leave you lost in sin,
Will not from here descend.

For if I listen to your jeers
And shun this tool of pain,
Who would open Heaven's gate?
Who your ransom gain?

Who would save beloved flock
From wolf that seeks to kill?
Who would lead my children home
To pastures green and still?

No, my dear, I won't come down.
I won't leave you alone.
No matter what you do to me,
I'll love to death my own.

And more than that, I'll freeze in time
This cruel, bloody, loss,
That veiled in bread, you feel my love
The same as from the cross.

No, I will not leave this cross.
I can't; love won't let go.
I want my sons, who caused this death,
My boundless love to know.

IMPELLING LOVE

A love, a love of God so near.
A love of God so pure and clear.
Impelling, compelling, oh who can say no?
Defenseless, our God such love here does show.
My Host, so silent, so humble, so meek.
My Host, my Host, no praises you seek,
Yet filling, renewing, and taking my thirst
'Til cup overflows and wineskins do burst.
Oh love without cause, this love unreturned,
Forgotten, unwanted, unnoticed and spurned.
Be moved, my poor heart, by this humble King,
And for those who won't, your love to him bring.

SILENT LOVER

Silent Lover, Gentle Host,
Why do you choose this way?
Infinite love you show to men,
Yet not a word you say.

Creator Lord, Eternal God,
Before we came to be,
You knew our face and called our name
And gave us light to see.

Silent Lover, Gentle Host,
You guide us as we grow.
Your take our little hand in yours;
The narrow way you show.

Gracious giver of all gifts:
Freedom, family, friends,
Vocation and those graces that
Your endless mercy sends.

Silent Lover, Gentle Host,
You came down from above.
All those years you lived on earth
To show Redemption's love.

Paschal Lamb, Victim Dear,
Your Passion and your death.
In finem[92] is your love for us
Until your dying breath.

Silent Lover, Gentle Host,
Could you have given more?
Yet you in Eucharist remain
That we may all adore.

Humble God, our hidden Lord,
'Til end of time you stay
With us behind those little doors
To comfort day by day.

Love unknown, ineffable love,
Oh Sacrament Divine,
Infinite love, you humble seek
In silence to confine.

Were it I, I'd shout it out,
Yet this is not God's way.
Silent Lover, Gentle Host,
Not a word you say.

Broken Heart

All my heart could ever seek,
My heart so wild, untame,
This human heart, this mystery
Of storm and ice and flame,
Is here within this holy place,
This sacrament of healing grace.

The voids, those dark and dampened voids
That pierce a groaning heart,
With no apparent reason why,

This heart is torn apart.
Irrational, this heart oft' blind,
No reason for these caverns find.

Oft' it feels alone and cold
Amid a joyous crowd,
And oft' it pines in emptiness
Before achievements proud,
As "water, water everywhere,"[93]
Yet not a drop of it to share.

Tired, angry, pressed for time,
My microcosm burns.
The dark sky falls, and I am worn
With heart my own self spurns.
A world in stress, yet world so small.
Still to my heart it seems as all.

Oh world so small, my foolish heart,
Though everything goes wrong,
Your God knows all and keeps you close,
His sheltering hand holds strong!
He longs to fill your throbbing need,
Your hung'ring soul with fullness feed.

All the love that heart can hold,
Affection, peace and rest,
Is here to sooth this bleeding one,
By childish worries pressed.
Great God on high is waiting here
To fill this heart in drawing near.

Come then, yes come, approach this well.
To where else will you go?
Here will heart be purely filled.
Here deep peace will know.
Christ is waiting, do not hide.
Come, and in his heart confide.

Beyond Me

Too much! My little heart cannot
Conceive what I receive,
And unawares of such a gift,
Almighty not perceive.

Routine, my nature's numbing drink,
Ne'er ceases soul to soak,
And blind to greatest majesty,
Fresh wonder slowly choke.

Routinely I receive him whole,
His full divinity,
His body and his blood, his soul,
Yet I too numbed to see.

Routinely I approach the greatest
Sacrifice of Love,
Perpetuated from the cross,
Where earth meets Heav'n above.

Yet Christ knows well my frailty,
My limits, my routine.

My childish world can't comprehend
What eyes of faith have seen.

He knows this is beyond me,
Yet how I long to raise
Unto this wondrous sacrament
Bouquet of flow'ring praise.

Undaunted by my poor return,
He chooses here to stay
In Eucharistic form with me
Until th' eternal day.

LOVE FROM BENEATH

My Love approaches from beneath
With purest, humble love.
Not as tyrant nor as lord
Who looks down from above.

Why do you, My Love, My God,
Draw near me from below
In silent form of harmless bread,
Your grandeur you forgo?

Gentle, soft, and unperceived,
Your eyes look up in mine.
This meeting gaze of begging Love
My coarsest heart refine.

You are God, yet in this form
I tower over you

That you may fit upon my tongue
And my whole soul imbue.

No pride in God Omnipotent,
In Eucharist made one,
Approaching, begging from beneath,
One with me his son.

With hands outstretched, to me you beg,
Though I should make this plea.
Who am I that you should stoop
Such depths to be with me?

Stay with Us

Stay with me, Lord.
How good to be here.
Though lonely I be,
You chose to be near.

Your child, whom my fear
And worries pursue,
Impelled by sick heart,
I come home to you.

I tremble and shake,
Afraid of the night,
Yet here I have you
To sweeten my plight.

Don't go, my Love,
Yet how can't you stay,
With no hands or feet
To take you away?

You want to be here
With no way to go,
That your risking love
For this son may show.

You prove to this child
That here you will be,
To comfort and hold
'Til eternity.

I Lay My Head

I lay my head upon your chest
As John on that night long ago.
In you my soul finds purest rest,
For you, my God, my heart all know.

You know my weakness and my shame,
And when I strike your loving face,
But you ne'er cease to call my name,
And beckon back to your embrace.

There's nothing I could ever do
To rip me from your caring arm.

Each time I come back rent to you,
You heal your child of chosen harm.

Yes, here is truly home for me,
This house wherein you with us dwell,
My peaceful soul can awing see
The love which eloquence can't tell.

Here let me live, here let me die,
My head upon your gentle chest,
For here on earth you truly lie,
Here a taste of Heaven's rest.

Chapter 8

HOME AT LAST

Oh Lord, why is it that we do not remember
that the reward is great and everlasting?[94]

† Teresa of Avila

We don't dream enough of Heaven. One day we will be there. It's hard to imagine. We forget that we are just passing through, that soon we will arrive to the dawn of that new and endless day when at last Christ will definitively conquer. One day we will enter into his fullest embrace, never to leave.

"Merely to look toward Heaven recollects the soul."[95] Our earthly life isn't the end but the journey. "Toward Heaven let us journey!"[96] There are struggles, but "the trials of this world, the rage of the devil, and the pains of Hell, are nothing to pass through, in order to plunge into this fathomless fountain of love."[97] To see the grandeur of this embrace to which he is pulling us would blind us. It's... too much, too good. Our Father is too good!

"Eye has not seen, and ear has not heard!"[98] Our pains will come to an end. Our "interior and exterior trials have been recompensed by the divine mercies, none of them being without its corresponding reward."[99] "So I say that if I were to be asked which I prefer, either to bear all the trials of the world until its end and afterward ascend to a little more glory or without any trials to descend to a little bit less, I would very eagerly choose all the trials for a little more of rejoicing in the knowledge of God's grandeurs."[100] It is all worth it!

We were made for Heaven, for his embrace. In this life, we enter more and more into his arms if we allow him to purify our hearts. We begin Heaven on earth.

"Through his favors we can understand something of what he will give us in Heaven without the intervals, trials, and dangers that there are in this tempestuous sea."[101] What an explosive, exciting, trusting, irrepressible joy this imprints on our lives! "It's natural that what is worth much costs much."[102] The pain of the road often so absorbs us, yet "all the trials suffered were well worth it."[103] "No wonder we have to pay what seems to us a high price. The time will come when you will understand how trifling everything is next to so precious a reward."[104]

"I have come home at last! This is my real country! I belong here. This is the land I have been looking for all my life, though I never knew it 'til now."[105]

The day is coming! Dream of it! Let him pull you in. The journey will end, and we will be home at last, home in his arms, never to leave this eternal embrace!

SILENT SHOES

A pair of weathered walking shoes
Lay offset at the door.
Old and tired, faded brown,
To journey on no more.

Through many years on many paths
Their load had loyal born,
And many miles of dusty trail
Have broken down and worn.

But now the master's gone away
Unto a new abode,
And he will journey on no more
At ending of the road.

For now his quest has gained its goal,
His travels now are done.
He reached the home toward which he strove,
Another life begun.

So there those faithful shoes may rest,
Peaceful on the floor.
Now no grind of painful path,
To journey on no more.

But whose, I ask, these silent shoes,
That from the road resign?
The lace and sole I recognize.
These silent shoes are mine.

Victory

A day will come when o'er the field
Of battle we will hear
A trumpet blast, and then at last
We'll see our King appear.

And soldiers from the dust will rise
Unto this glorious sound,
And brandish sword unto the King
In victory now crowned.

Those legions vast of soldiers brave,
Who stood within the breach
As Hell broke loose and victory seemed
Beyond all hopeful reach.

These soldiers now arise and come
To banner of the King,
Assembled vast, this glorious host
That hymn of triumph sing.

Fear not, this day will surely come,
Though darkened battle now.
Fight brave, that on that dawn you may
Before the Victor bow.

Fields More Fertile Still[106]

With calloused hand he reaches down
To ruffle dusty peat,

A man that knew the soil's song
And nature's subtle beat.

Those hilly fields along that road,
He knew them through and through.
So many seasons, many crops,
He cared for as they grew.

A simple man who walked these fields
To sew and reap and till,
Yet other fields now call him on,
Fields more fertile still.

He leaves behind a legacy,
A family and a farm,
An open gap that can't be filled,
A smile, a laugh, a charm.

His dusted cap of faded green,
Those boots on which he'd roam
A thousand miles yet ne'er abroad,
On selfsame fields of home.

The herd he built, the sheds he raised,
The tractors and the bales,
The bins and barns, the lots and yards,
The augers and the pales.

The black and white that marked his life,
The oats, the corn, the hay,
They all will miss his constant care,
Now taken far away.

Yet greener fields now call him on,
That need a farmer's hand,
And knowing he'd been farming long,
They've beckoned to this land.

Yes, He, the greatest farming hand,
Who made those very rows,
Has called to rest close by his side
This worn man who now goes.

Enjoy those fields, dear farmer.
Enjoy the Lord's embrace.
You fought the fight. You finished well.
You've strongly run the race.

You ne'er did stop your work below.
Now it's time to rest
On farm where you were meant to be,
Fore'er in Heaven blest.

That glory day has dawned for you,
To other wagons fill
In greener fields than these below,
Fields more fertile still.

HOME AT LAST

I lay there on that grassy hill.
Where? I didn't know.
But bare sun shone upon my face,
And gentle breeze did blow.

The morning dove cooed out her note.
I heard a whistling stream.
Without a hint of where I was,
Reality or dream.

I slowly opened up my eyes
And saw sun's blinding light.
With aching arms, I propped myself,
And viewed a valley bright.

Far off blue mountains stretched abroad,
Below a humming brook,
And flowers painted all around
That hill where I did look.

My gaze then fell upon myself,
All clad in battle gear.
Some epic battle must have raged,
And I had fallen here.

All bruised and caked with dust and blood,
I lay there in that field.
Upon my right a splintered sword,
My left, a battered shield.

A soldier then walked up to me,
Meek, yet in command.
He greeted me with soft, deep voice
And reached to me his hand.

"Well done, my brother warrior.
You've finished well the fight.

When everything seemed dark and lost,
You ne'er forgot the light.

"Now let me take you to our King,
That you your Lord may greet."
So Michael spoke with outstretched hand
And pulled me to my feet.

Then leaning on his shoulder firm,
I limped down from that hill,
And at the base we came across
A gently singing rill.

He bade me lay aside my gear,
I needed it no more,
And wash away the sweat and blood
And dust from every pore.

And when that water washed me clean,
It took away my pain.
So then my aching body now
Refreshed and strong again.

He dressed me in a garment new,
A robe of silken white,
No more to stain with sweat and strife
As oft' amid the fight.

He said, "Now let me take you home
Unto your just reward.
My brother, let us onward
To the dwelling of the Lord."

Along that stream he led me
O'er hills and prairies green,
Through light-filled forest lush with life,
Of beauty yet unseen.

Until we came unto the gates
Whence blinding light gushed out,
And when those doors rolled open wide,
There rang a glorious shout.

I tried to catch my senses, numb,
So deafened by the cry,
And squinting through the blinding light,
I saw before me lie

A host of men and women there,
As far as eye could see,
Sending out a deafening shout,
Cheering there for me.

"These the souls that by your love
Our Lord could save through you."
St Michael spoke these words to me
As dumbstruck I passed through.

And at the end of that great host
On left and on the right,
A group of men and women brave
Who shared with me the fight.

These the fellow warriors,
Who'd given all and more,

Faithful in the line of fire,
Brothers gone before.

They clapped for me with smile serene,
A warm embrace from each.
They who helped by work and prayer
This glorious place to reach.

Side by side on earth we fought;
Now side by side we'll stand
With one accord him to adore,
As we had done on earth before,
But now in glory evermore
In this triumphant land.

Then on my shoulder Michael tapped
And pointed with his hand.
Beyond these men and women there
Did Mother Mary stand.

I stood there frozen, couldn't move.
My heart, it heav'ly beat.
My gaze and hers, they firmly locked.
At last our eyes did meet.

I felt a warmth pulse through my veins
As eyes filled up with tears.
Now at last that first embrace
I'd longed for all these years.

I never wanted it to end,
That eternal maternal embrace.

A timeless length she held me there,
Enveloped by her grace.

"Welcome home, my little one.
Your lifelong journey now is done.
Eternal joy at last begun.
Let me lead you to my Son."

So she spoke, and with her hand
Upon my back with love,
She led me past the cheering crowd
Up singing stairs above.

Up I walked those iv'ry steps,
Flanked with cherubim bright
On either side with glowing joy,
And burst of seraph's might.

Most glorious choir that e'er was heard,
Exultant flood of praise,
A booming chorus loud resounds,
Triumphant voices raise.

Atop those shining stairs we stood.
I saw a golden throne.
And coming from that glorious seat,
A blinding light was shone.

Around it stood an angel host,
A voiceless glory's sight,
Singing out the victory hymn,
Clothed in robes of light.

And at the foot of beaming throne,
My eyes filled up with tears,
For there he stood, the one for whom
I'd longed for all these years.

"My Jesus, My Jesus, My Jesus, Love!
Is it really you?"
A moment I just stood and looked.
At last, can it be true?

Is the battle really done?
Is the victory finally won?
Have I come at last to rest
With the host of all the Blessed?

In faith through fog I longed to come,
But ne'er imagined when.
Is long-awaited moment here
That I had hoped for then?

Out of my daze I snapped and ran
Unto the Eternal Son,
And he to me with open arms
To prodigal did run.

Now at last the first embrace
That Jesus gave to me.
For many years I'd dreamed of how
This coming home would be.

An eternity we stayed there.
He couldn't let me go.

There were so…so…so… many things
I wanted him to know.

Yet not a word came from my mouth,
So filled with joy was I.
Motionless we there embraced,
Eternity flowed by.

After all those years in which
I'd run my earthly race,
What I dreamed to say to him
When I beheld his face?

I'd tell him all the things I'd done,
The laughter and the pain,
The joys and sorrows, trials and sweat,
The losses and the gain.

But all that came in that embrace
Was "Jesus, I love you."
And with smile that melted gold,
He warmly said, "Me too."

"I've long awaited your coming here
When fight at last is fought.
Now look around at all the souls
That heavenward you brought."

And as I turned around and looked
And saw the cheering crowd,
Worth it all to bring them here,
To make my Jesus proud.

Worth the years of waiting cold,
The struggle day by day,
The hidden things that no one saw,
The silent prayers I'd pray.

Worth the cutting through the ice,
When all was dark and dim,
When all that kept me going was
A simple faith in him.

When all my work came crumbling down,
What sweat and blood had bought,
And what it took me years to build,
O'ernight reduced to naught.

Worth it all, the fight, the fall,
No matter to what it came.
He wanted just the love I showed.
The rest was all the same.

"Stay the course, my brother!"
I want to say to each.
Worth the struggles life can give
When final home you reach.

And when that final battle comes,
And with your wounds you fall,
How great will be your recompense
If you have given all.

It's worth it all, for on that day
Those victory words employ,

"Well done, good and faithful son,
Your lifelong race at last is run;
The war now waged, the battle done,
And you the victor's crown have won;
Now share your master's joy."

Appendix

The book is intended to be an aid to prayer and contemplation of the wonderful ways of God. As has been said, there is no strict linear progression of the poems. However, I have indicated a few "overtones" that occur in the various chapters as well as a simple index of virtues to help someone looking for a particular theme or sentiment in prayer.

Chapter Overtones

1. **Stinging Arrow**: longing for God, coping with our human frailty and sinfulness, anxiety, mercy, conversion, prayer, union with God and contemplation, intimacy with the Lord.

2. **Identity**: peace, filial trust, security in God's faithful Fatherly love, hope, simplicity, humility.

3. **Journey**: time and eternity, hope, perseverance, Heaven, vocation.

4. **Lead Me Blind**: faith, hope, trust, perseverance, abandonment, confusion, darkness, dryness.

5. **Gifts of the Wayside**: gratitude, wonder, joy, beauty.

6. **Dark Valleys**: hope, perseverance, darkness, suffering, dryness, cross, difficulties, trust.

7. **Companion**: God's personal love, gratitude, union with God, humility, wonder, peace, hope, consolation, contemplation, prayer, trust.

8. **Home at Last**: hope, perseverance, Heaven, joy, time and eternity.

Virtue Index

(The reference indicates the chapter in which the poem is found.)

abandonment: Father's Wish (2), Fear Not (2), Why This Road (4), Let God Lead (4), Unknown Way (4)

adoration: Glory Be (2), Look Beyond (5), The Whirlwind (5)

anxiety: My Only Need (1), How Long, My Love (1), Take Away (6), Slippery Slope (6), Only Him (7), Broken Heart (7), Stay with Us (7)

beauty: Baptismal Beauty (2), Unseen 'til Now (3), Look Beyond (5)

charity: Open Gaze (7)

confusion: Her Journey Home to Me (3), Lead Me Blind (4), Why This Road (4), All Will Be Okay (4)

consolation in God: Sweet Desert (1), Lost in the Sea of Love (1), Rest (1), Advanceless Gain (6), Can't Go On (6), Only Him (7), Broken Heart (7), Love from Beneath (7), Stay with Us (7), I Lay My Head (7)

contemplation: Sweet Desert (1), Silence (3), Stay with Us (7), I Lay My Head (7)

conversion: Come Instead to Me (1), My Only Need (1), Love to the Ungrateful (2), North Star (4)

courage: Fear Not (2)

cross: Unknown Fear (4)

darkness: Her Journey Home to Me (3), Lead Me Blind (4), Why This Road (4), Hidden Star (4), The Icebreaker (6), The Well (6), Numbed Soul (6), Slippery Slope (6)

desire for God: Sweet Desert (1), Come Instead to Me (1), Freeing Fetters (1), Consuming Fire (1), How Long, My Love (1), Stinging Arrow (1), God's Time (4), Take Away (6), My Burning Need (7), Sole Desire (7), Broken Heart (7), Stay with Us (7)

detachment: How Long, My Love (1), Rest (1), Just Passing Through (3)

docility: Channel (2), Her Journey Home to Me (3), Why This Road (4)

dryness: Lead Me Blind (4), The Icebreaker (6), Can't Go On (6), Numbed Soul (6), Slippery Slope (6)

Eucharist: The Whirlwind (5), The Stream (5), Irresistible (5), So Much More (5), Silent Lover (7), Broken Heart (7), Beyond Me (7), Love from Beneath (7), Stay with Us (7)

failure: North Star (4), Look Beyond (5), Advanceless Gain (6)

faith: Wisdom's Care (3), Lead Me Blind (4), Why This Road (4), Hidden Star (4), Fog (4), North Star (4)

fortitude: The Icebreaker (6), Advanceless Gain (6)

God's Love: Selfless Tears (2), Priceless Gift (5), Unfathomed Gift (5), Why Then (5), The Whirlwind (5),

The Stream (5), So Much More (5), My Burning Need (7), Sole Desire (7), Open Gaze (7), Come Off the Cross (7), Impelling Love (7), Stay with Us (7), I Lay My Head (7)

grace: Baptismal Beauty (2)

gratitude: Unseen 'til Now (3), Priceless Gift (5), Unn fathomed Gift (5), Oh Emmanuel (5), Undeserved Redemption (5), Gift of Gold (5), Beyond Me (7), Silent Lover (7), Love from Beneath (7)

Heaven: Just Passing Through (3), Her Journey Home to Me (3), Silent Shoes (8), Victory (8), Fields More Fertile Still (8), Home at Last (8)

hope: How Long, My Love (1), I Belong to You (2), Just Passing Through (3), Her Journey Home to Me (3), Lead Me Blind (4), Why This Road (4), All Will Be Okay (4), Fog (4), Unknown Way (4), The Well (6), Can't Go On (6), Numbed Soul (6), Slippery Slope (6), My Burning Need (7), Sole Desire (7), Victory (8), Home at Last (8)

humility: Father's Wish (2), Channel (2), Wisdom's Care (3), Priceless Gift (5), Infinite Mercy (5), Slippery Slope (6), Silent Lover (7), Love from Beneath (7)

Incarnation: Unfathomed Gift (5), Oh Emmanuel (5), Why Then (5), So Much More (5), Advanceless Gain (6), My Burning Need (7), Sole Desire (7)

interior division: Come Instead to Me (1), Freeing Fetters (1), Stinging Arrow (1), I Belong to You (2), Advanceless Gain (6), Take Away (6)

intimacy: Sweet Desert (1), Consuming Fire (1), Pull Me In (1), Lost in the Sea of Love (1), Stinging Arrow (1), Only Him (7)

mercy: Selfless Tears (2), Love to the Ungrateful (2), Undeserved Redemption (5), The Stream (5), Infinite Mercy (5), Open Gaze (7), Come Off the Cross (7), Impelling Love (7), I Lay My Head (7)

need: My Only Need (1), Only Him (7), My Burning Need (7), Sole Desire (7), Broken Heart (7)

patience: How Long, My Love (1), God's Time (4), Advanceless Gain (6), Open Gaze (7)

peace: Rest (1), Identity (2), Father's Wish (2), Fear Not (2), God's Embrace (2), Let God Lead (4), All Will Be Okay (4), Infinite Mercy (5), Only Him (7), I Lay My Head (7)

perseverance: Her Journey Home to Me (3), Lead Me Blind (4), God's Time (4), The Icebreaker (6), Advanceless Gain (6), Can't Go On (6), Numbed Soul (6), Slippery Slope (6), Victory (8), Home at Last (8)

prayer: Irresistible (5), Slippery Slope (6), Stay with Us (7), I Lay My Head (7)

purification: Freeing Fetters (1), How Long, My Love (1), My Only Need (1), Wisdom's Care (3), Lead Me Blind (4), Take Away (6)

trust: My Only Need (1), Identity (2), I Belong to You (2), Father's Wish (2), Fear Not (2), Selfless Tears (2), God's Embrace (2), Wisdom's Care (3), Her Journey Home to Me (3), Let God Lead (4), All Will Be Okay (4), Unknown Fear (4), God's Time (4), Unknown Way (4), Infinite Mercy (5), The Icebreaker (6), Numbed Soul (6), Slippery Slope (6), Only Him (7), Beyond Me (7)

understanding: Just Passing Through (3)

union with God: Sweet Desert (1), Come Instead to Me (1), Freeing Fetters (1), Consuming Fire (1), Pull Me In (1), Lost in the Sea of Love (1), Baptismal Beauty (2), Silence (3), Irresistible (5), So Much More (5), Only Him (7), Beyond Me (7), Love from Beneath (7), Stay with Us (7)

vocation: Sweet Desert (1), Channel (2), Her Journey Home to Me (3)

weakness: Freeing Fetters (1), Can't Go On (6), Numbed Soul (6), Take Away (6), Slippery Slope (6)

wonder: Unseen 'til Now (3), Look Beyond (5), Unfathomed Gift (5), Oh Emmanuel (5), Why Then (5), Gift of Gold (5), So Much More (5), Infinite Mercy (5), Impelling Love (7), Silent Lover (7), Beyond Me (7), Love from Beneath (7)

worries: Only Him (7), Broken Heart (7), Stay with Us (7), I Lay My Head (7)

REFERENCES

Quotes of St Teresa of Avila are taken from *The Collected Works of Teresa of Avila, Vol I-III*, ICS Publications, translated by Kieran Kavanaugh, OCD, and Otilio Rodriguez, OCD, Washington DC, 1980.

Quotes of St John of the Cross are taken from *The Complete Work of Saint John of the Cross, Vol I-II,* Waxkeep Publishing, translated by the Oblate Fathers of St Charles, 2015.

Biblical quotes are taken from *The New American Bible,* World Bible Publishers, Inc., Iowa Falls, 1987.

[1] JOHN OF THE CROSS, *Vol I*, pg 201, The Ascent of Mount Carmel, bk 2, ch 26, paragraph 8-9.

[2] JOHN OF THE CROSS, *Vol I*, pg 201, The Ascent of Mount Carmel, bk 2, ch 26, paragraph 6.

[3] TERESA OF AVILA, *Vol II*, pg 242, Meditations on the Song of Songs, ch 3, paragraph 14.

[4] FRANCIS, Message of His Holiness Pope Francis for the 51st World Communications Day, Vatican, January 24, 2017.

[5] MARGARET MARY ALAQUOQUE, Message of the Sacred Heart to St Margaret Mary Alaquoque, First Apparition, December 27, 1673.

[6] JOHN OF THE CROSS, *Vol I*, pg 194, The Ascent of Mount Carmel, bk 2, ch 24, paragraph 4.

[7] Matthew 11:17.

[8] JOHN OF THE CROSS, *Vol II*, pg 13, Spiritual Canticle between the Soul and Christ, stanza 15.

[9] Hosea 2:14.

[10] John 14:3.

[11] JOHN OF THE CROSS, *The Collected Works of Saint John of the Cross,* Revised Edition, ICS Publications, translated by Kieran Kavanaugh, OCD, and Otilio Rodriguez, OCD, Washington DC, 1991, pg 45, Spiritual Canticle between the Soul and Christ, stanzas 8-9.

[12] Augustine, *Confessions*, bk I, i, 1.

[13] Romans 7:15.

[14] John of the Cross, *Vol II*, pg 209, The Living Flame of Love, stanza 1-2.

[15] Teresa of Avila, *Vol II*, pg 368, The Interior Castle, Dwelling VI, ch 2, paragraph 4.

[16] John of the Cross, *Vol II*, pg 230, The Living Flame of Love, stanza 2, paragraph 3.

[17] John of the Cross, *Vol II*, pg 227, The Living Flame of Love, stanza 2, paragraph 2.

[18] Teresa of Avila, *Vol III*, pg 379, poem 3.

[19] Psalm 38:3.

[20] John of the Cross, *Vol II*, pg 12, Spiritual Canticle between the Soul and Christ, stanzas 8-9.

[21] Song of Songs 3:3.

[22] Teresa of Avila, *Vol III*, pg 405, poem 28.

[23] Teresa of Avila, *Vol III*, pg 280, poem 3.

[24] Teresa of Avila, *Vol III*, pg 277, poem 2.

[25] Luke 15:11-32.

[26] Teresa of Avila, *Vol III*, pg 379, poem 3.

[27] John of the Cross, *Vol II*, pg 243, The Living Flame of Love, stanza 3, paragraph 1.

[28] Teresa of Avila, prayer attributed to her.

[29] Psalm 23:1.

[30] *In finem*: (Latin) "until the end" (Jn 13:1).

[31] Teresa of Avila, *Vol II*, pg 117, The Way of Perfection, ch 21, paragraph 1.

[32] John of the Cross, *Vol II*, pg 311, Letter 13: To the Lady Joanna de Pedraça.

[33] Teresa of Avila, *Vol II*, pg 151, The Way of Perfection, ch 30, paragraph 6.

[34] Teresa of Avila, *Vol II*, pg 114, The Way of Perfection, ch 20, paragraph 2.

[35] Billy Graham, quote attributed to him.

[36] *Gaudium et Spes,* Holy See Webpage, paragraph 57.

[37] Teresa of Avila, *Vol III*, pg 403, poem 26.

[38] Luke 24:13-35.

[39] Psalm 44:25.

[40] TERESA OF AVILA, *Vol II*, pg 431, Interior Castle, Dwelling VII, ch 1, paragraph 9.

[41] Luke 24:13-35.

[42] Isaiah 55:9.

[43] JOHN OF THE CROSS, *Vol I*, pg 450, The Dark Night, bk 2, ch 21, paragraph 5.

[44] Psalm 139:11.

[45] Psalm 139:12.

[46] ANNE-MARIE PELLETIER, *Meditations for the Good Friday Way of the Cross with Pope Francis,* published by the Office of the Liturgical Celebrations of the Supreme Pontiff, April 14, 2017, Eleventh Station, pg 52. The English translation is my own of the original Italian.

[47] JOHN HENRY NEWMAN, "Lead Kindly Light", 1833.

[48] TERESA OF AVILA, *Vol II*, pg 216, Meditations on the Song of Songs, ch 1, paragraph 1.

[49] JOHN OF THE CROSS, *Vol II*, pg 311, Letter 13: To the Lady Joanna de Pedraça.

[50] JOHN OF THE CROSS, *Vol II*, pg 311, Letter 13: To the Lady Joanna de Pedraça.

[51] TERESA OF AVILA, *Vol III*, pg 386, poem 9.

[52] TERESA OF AVILA, *Vol I*, pg 253, The Book of Her Life, ch 29, paragraph 14.

[53] John 4:10.

[54] TERESA OF AVILA, *Vol I*, pg 158-159, The Book of Her Life, ch 18, paragraph 4.

[55] JOHN OF THE CROSS, *Vol II*, pg 42, Spiritual Canticle between the Soul and Christ, stanza 6, Introduction.

[56] JOHN OF THE CROSS, *Vol II*, pg 42, Spiritual Canticle between the Soul and Christ, stanza 6, Introduction.

[57] JOHN OF THE CROSS, *Vol II*, pg 201, Spiritual Canticle between the Soul and Christ, stanza 39, paragraph 11.

[58] TERESA OF AVILA, *Vol I*, pg 321, The Book of Her Life, ch 36, paragraph 27.

[59] Mark 8:34.

[60] TERESA OF AVILA, *Vol III*, pg 395, poem 19.

[61] TERESA OF AVILA, *Vol II*, pg 240, Meditations on the Song of Songs, ch 3, paragraph 10.

[62] Maria Faustina Kowalska, *Diary, Divine Mercy in my Soul*, Marian Press, Stockbridge, MA, Third Edition, 2004, paragraph 1804, pg 638.

[63] Teresa of Avila, *Vol II*, pg 162, The Way of Perfection, ch 32, paragraph 7.

[64] Psalm 119:71.

[65] Isaiah 53:3.

[66] Teresa of Avila, *Vol II*, pg 362, Interior Castle, Dwelling VI, ch 1, paragraph 7.

[67] Sirach 2:5.

[68] John of the Cross, *Vol II*, pg 233, The Living Flame of Love, stanza 5, paragraph 3.

[69] Teresa of Avila, *Vol I*, pg 115-116, The Book of Her Life, ch 11, paragraph 11.

[70] Teresa of Avila, *Vol III*, pg 394, poem 18.

[71] John of the Cross, *Vol II*, pg 230, The Living Flame of Love, stanza II, paragraph 3.

[72] Teresa of Avila, *Vol II*, pg 378, Interior Castle, Dwelling VI, ch 4, paragraph 1.

[73] Teresa of Avila, *Vol II*, pg 251, Meditations on the Song of Songs, ch 6, paragraph 2.

[74] Teresa of Avila, *Vol I*, pg 286, The Book of Her Life, ch 33, paragraph 4.

[75] Teresa of Avila, *Vol II*, pg 259, Meditations on the Song of Songs, ch 7, paragraph 8.

[76] Teresa of Avila, *Vol II*, pg 185, The Way of Perfection, ch 38, paragraph 1.

[77] Teresa of Avila, *Vol II*, pg 101, The Way of Perfection, ch 17, paragraph 7.

[78] Teresa of Avila, *Vol I*, pg 313, The Book of Her Life, ch 36, paragraph 9.

[79] Teresa of Avila, *Vol II*, pg 181, The Way of Perfection, ch 36, paragraph 8.

[80] Revelation 21:4.

[81] Teresa of Avila, *Vol II*, pg 241, Meditations on the Song of Songs, ch 3, paragraph 12.

[82] Teresa of Avila, *Vol II*, pg 246, Meditations on the Song of Songs, ch 4, paragraph 9.

[83] Luke 24:29.

[84] Matthew 28:20.

[85] TERESA OF AVILA, *Vol III*, pg 386, poem 9.

[86] Psalm 23:4.

[87] Hebrews 4:15.

[88] Isaiah 53:4.

[89] TERESA OF AVILA, *Vol I*, pg 194, The Book of Her Life, ch 22, paragraph 6.

[90] TERESA OF AVILA, *Vol II*, pg 50, The Way of Perfection, ch 3, paragraph 6.

[91] Matthew 14:31.

[92] *In finem*: (Latin) "until the end" (Jn 13:1).

[93] SAMUEL TAYLOR COLERIDGE, "Rime of the Ancient Mariner", part II, stanza 9.

[94] TERESA OF AVILA, *Vol II*, pg 230, Meditations on the Song of Songs, ch 2, paragraph 17.

[95] TERESA OF AVILA, *Vol I*, pg 332, The Book of Her Life, ch 38, paragraph 6.

[96] TERESA OF AVILA, *Vol III*, pg 386, poem 10.

[97] JOHN OF THE CROSS, *Vol II*, pg 68, Spiritual Canticle between the Soul and Christ, stanza 13, Introduction.

[98] 1 Corinthians 2:9.

[99] JOHN OF THE CROSS, *Vol II*, pg 236, The Living Flame of Love, Stanza II, paragraph 5.

[100] TERESA OF AVILA, *Vol I*, pg 323-324, The Book of Her Life, ch 37, paragraph 2.

[101] TERESA OF AVILA, *Vol II*, pg 353, Interior Castle, Dwelling V, ch 4, paragraph 11.

[102] TERESA OF AVILA, *Vol II*, pg 424, Interior Castle, Dwelling VI, ch 11, paragraph 6.

[103] TERESA OF AVILA, *Vol I*, pg 321, The Book of Her Life, ch 36, paragraph 27.

[104] TERESA OF AVILA, *Vol II*, pg 117, The Way of Perfection, ch 21, paragraph 1.

[105] C.S. LEWIS, *The Last Battle*, Collier Books, Division of Macmillan Publishing Co, Inc, New York, 1979, ch 15, pg 171.

[106] Written on the death of my grandfather, Donald Scherber.

Made in the USA
Coppell, TX
03 November 2020

40717349R00089